Ripley's Believe It or Not!®

**Developed and produced by Ripley Publishing Ltd**

This edition published and distributed by:

Mason Crest
370 Reed Road, Broomall, Pennsylvania 19008
www.masoncrest.com

Printed and bound in the United States of America.

First printing
9 8 7 6 5 4 3 2 1

Ripley's Believe It or Not!
Body Bizarre
ISBN-13: 978-1-4222-2563-9 (hardcover)
ISBN-13: 978-1-4222-9238-9 (e-book)
Ripley's Believe It or Not!—Complete 16 Title Series
ISBN-13: 978-1-4222-2560-8

Library of Congress Cataloging-in-Publication Data

Body bizarre.
    p. cm. – (Ripley's believe it or not!)
 ISBN 978-1-4222-2563-9 (hardcover) – ISBN 978-1-4222-2560-8 (series hardcover) –
ISBN 978-1-4222-9238-9 (ebook)
1. Human body–Social aspects–Juvenile literature. 2. Abnormalities, Human–Juvenile literature.
 GT495.P74 2012
 599.9'49–dc23
                        2012020334

PUBLISHER'S NOTE
While every effort has been made to verify the accuracy of the entries in this book, the Publisher's cannot be held responsible for any errors contained in the work. They would be glad to receive any information from readers.

WARNING
Some of the stunts and activities in this book are undertaken by experts and should not be attempted by anyone without adequate training and supervision.

# Ripley's Believe It or Not!

## Disbelief and Shock!

# BODY BIZARRE

www.MasonCrest.com

# BODY BIZARRE

Wonderfully weird. You won't believe just how

amazing the human body can be. Read about

someone who can charge lightbulbs through his

head and ears, a man who has been eating live

frogs to cure his coughs for 40 years, and another

who has permanently blue skin.

*Laura Chadwick's human art transforms
the body into a canvas.*

# SHOCKING!

**Zhang Deke can use his power as a human conductor of electricity to charge six 13-watt lightbulbs simply by placing them on his head and ears.**

As the bulbs light up, he is even able to control their brightness. He has also cooked a fish, which he held in his hand as the current flowed through his body, in just two minutes!

Zhang, 71, a retired highway maintenance worker from Altay City, China, often exercises by hooking himself up to the electricity supply. With both hands holding live wires, he allows 220 volts of electricity to run through his body without any ill effects, even though it is the same charge that an electric eel delivers to kill a human.

He first discovered his extraordinary ability when he was 47. While changing a lightbulb, he accidentally touched a live wire, but instead of receiving a shock or being electrocuted, he felt almost nothing. He tentatively tried it again and eventually realized that his body could conduct electricity. In 1994, he was examined at the Chinese Academy of Sciences, where experts said he has an unspecified physical dysfunction.

Zhang administers his electrical therapy to help friends and relatives who are suffering from ailments such as rheumatism, arthritis, and lumbago. One friend had been bedridden for some time with lumbar hyperplasia, but nine months after receiving Zhang's shock treatment he was out riding a bicycle.

*Zhang's incredible capacity to cook a fish with his body's electric current has amazed the world.*

*Zhang demonstrates his electrical abilities by lighting up a string of lightbulbs being worn by a friend.*

## Other shockers!

● Whenever Angélique Cottin, the "Electric Girl" of 19th-century France, went near an object, it moved away from her. Chairs twisted away from her when she tried to sit down, a heavy table rose into the air when she touched it, and if she tried to sleep in a bed, it rocked violently. People standing near her received electric shocks without her even touching them.

● Annie May Abbott, "The Little Georgia Magnet," toured the world demonstrating her ability to raise a chair with a heavy man seated on it, apparently just by touching it with her hand.

● Caroline Clare of Ontario, Canada, developed electrical powers soon after dramatically losing weight. Metal objects would jump into her hand and she gave an electric shock to anyone she touched. In one experiment, she passed a shock down a line of 20 people who were holding hands.

● When the fingertips of Louis Hamburger, a 16-year-old student from Maryland, were dry, he could pick up heavy objects simply by touching them. Pins dangled from his open hand as if they were hanging from a magnet.

● Brian Clements of the U.K., was so highly charged that he had to discharge his voltage into metal furniture before he touched anyone.

● Brenda Sheklian of Visalia, California, says that street lamps turn off when she passes under them and switch back on when she moves away. She also claims that her electrical powers can turn off the TV, blow lightbulbs, and freeze her computer.

### RIPLEY'S research ○○○○○○○○○

**How can some people possess special electric powers?**

The human nervous system actually generates electricity. When we walk across a thick carpet, our body can build up around 10,000 volts, but because it can actually develop only a small electrical charge, the discharged current is equally insignificant. Yet so-called "electric people" are sometimes able to maximize their electrical potential.

Doctors believe that the ability to conduct electricity may be governed by a person's health and becomes more marked in the aftermath of a serious illness or disease. Other case studies suggest that the climate is responsible, with electrical activity at its liveliest during a heat wave. As yet, however, there are no definitive answers to a puzzle that has perplexed medical minds for more than 150 years.

*The "Electric Man," Zhang Deke, all lit up.*

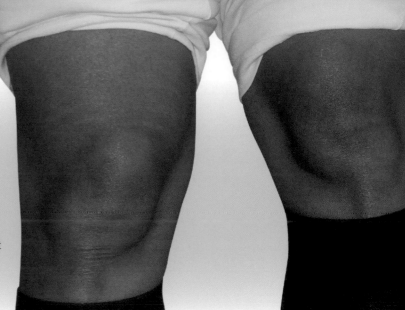

## KNEE IMAGES

In December 2006, Amia Fore of Detroit, Michigan, was amazed when she looked in the mirror and saw what appeared to be a face on her right kneecap. A month later another "face" appeared—this time on her left kneecap, the features becoming more pronounced as the weeks passed. A spiritual advisor said the initial image was of Amia's first (unborn) grandchild and that the features would disappear once the baby was born.

### HUMAN MAGNET

Romanian Aurel Raileanu often finds himself literally glued to the television. The Bucharest hospital worker has become known as the Human Magnet because spoons, books, lighters, and even a 50-lb (23-kg) TV set, all stick to him.

### SWOLLEN FINGERS

Liu Hua from Jiangsu Province, China, had fingers that were thicker than his arms. His left thumb, index finger, and middle finger were deformed at birth and grew to a huge size before surgeons removed 11 lb (5 kg) of bone and tissue from them in 2007.

### PENGUIN GIRL

As she had no forearms, only three toes on each foot, and a distinctive walk, diminutive Nany Mae Hill of Keyes, California, was billed in circus shows as the "Penguin Girl". After marrying 6-ft-tall (2.2-m) farmer Benjamin Hill in the 1940s, she wore her wedding ring on the middle toe of her left foot.

### LEGLESS ACROBAT

Born in Ohio in 1844, Eli Bowen had no legs—just two small feet of different sizes growing from his hips. As a toddler, he used his arms for walking and would hold wooden blocks in his hands, enabling him to swing his hips between his arms. The strength he developed from walking in this manner helped him become a top-class acrobat.

### SEAL AND CHIMP

Stanislaus Berent of Pittsburgh, Pennsylvania, had hands growing from his shoulders, but no arms—a condition known as phocomelia. Billed in shows as "Sealo the Seal Boy," his act featured a chimpanzee to which he fed cookies.

### ROLE MODEL

Firefighter John Joseph Conway from Chicago, Illinois, underwent plastic surgery in India to make himself look like Hollywood star Bruce Willis. He spent $1,600 on the operation because he thought Willis' strong jaw was the ideal look for a firefighter.

### LOBSTER BOY

Born in 1937, Grady Stiles Jr. from Pittsburgh, Pennsylvania, suffered from ectrodactyly, where the fingers are fused together in groups to form claw-like extremities. Consequently, he was billed in shows as "Lobster Boy."

### Ripley's research

Yu Zhenhuan suffers from hypertrichosis—or werewolf syndrome—a condition that produces excessive body hair. He has 256 hairs growing on almost every square inch of his skin. The condition is usually genetic and occurs in around one out of every ten billion people.

### BODY HAIR

Yu Zhenhuan has thick hair covering 96 percent of his entire body—every inch except for the palms of his hands and the soles of his feet. His eyelashes are so long that they hide his eyes. Also known in his native China as rock singer King Kong, Yu has undergone five operations to remove hair from his nose and recently had another to remove a clump of hair from his ear because it was impairing his hearing.

## HORNED MAN

*An 88-year-old man from a village near Zhengzhou, China, has a horn growing from his head. It started in 2006 when he picked at a little bump on his head and it went on to grow steadily over the next few months. Doctors believe it is a form of hyperplasia, an excess of normal body tissue.*

### HAIR MOP

Thousands of prisoners donated their hair to help soak up spilled fuel following the crash of an oil tanker off the coast of the Philippines in August 2006.

### BLADDER STONE

Doctors in Israel removed a bladder stone from Moneera Khalil that was the size of a grapefruit! The stone measured 5 1/8 in (13 cm) across and weighed nearly 2 lb 4 oz (1 kg).

### EXTRA LIMBS

Rudy Santos of Bacolad City, the Philippines, has been promoted as "Octoman" on account of having three legs and four arms. One of the legs is missing below the knee and he also has the small head and ear of his parasitic twin attached to his stomach.

### MASSIVE TUMOR

Huang Chuncai, 31, of Hunan, China, is only 4 ft 6 in (1.37 m) tall but he had a facial tumor that was nearly 2 ft (60 cm) long and weighed 33 lb (15 kg). It first appeared when he was four and grew so rapidly that it blocked his left eye, pushed his left ear down to shoulder level, knocked out his teeth, and deformed his backbone. By the time the tumor was removed in 2007, it was hanging down from his face.

### QUARTER BOY

Johnny Gilmore—alias "Zandu the Quarter Boy"—was born in Marshalltown, Iowa, in 1913 with the entire lower part of his body missing. He used to walk on his hands.

### STRANGE COUPLE

Percilla Lauther from Puerto Rico had a hormonal imbalance that left her with a dark beard and hair all over her body. She was billed in shows as "Priscilla the Monkey Girl" and in 1938 she eloped with performer Emmitt Bejano, "The Alligator-Skinned Boy," who suffered from ichthyosis, giving him scaly skin. Together they were promoted as "The World's Strangest Married Couple."

### BABY TEETH

A baby in England was born in 2007 with teeth. Megan Andrews from Worthing, Sussex, stunned family by arriving in the world with seven teeth.

# Tattoo Master

At InkLine Studio in New York City, Anil Gupta can reproduce a famous artwork as a tattoo without losing any of the intricate detail from the original painting. He has created postage-stamp-size tattoos of works by Michelangelo, Van Gogh, and Leonardo da Vinci, including a tiny copy of the *Mona Lisa* and this shoulder-width version of *The Last Supper*.

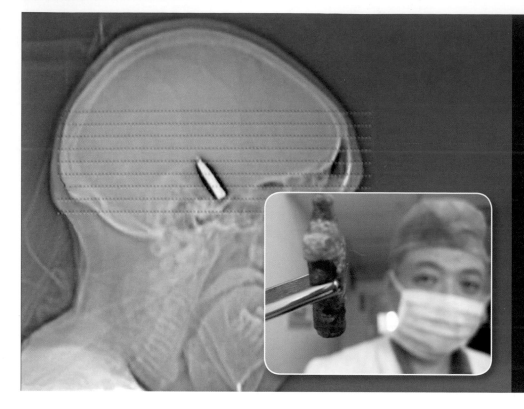

## LONG SHOT

In 2007, a Chinese grandmother finally discovered the cause of the recurrent headaches she had been suffering for 64 years—a bullet had been lodged in her skull since 1943.

Jin Guangying was just 13 when she was shot in the head by the Japanese army while delivering lunch to her father, a soldier stationed in Jiangsu Province. Although she recovered from her ordeal, she went on to experience repeated headaches, during which she would babble incoherently, pound her head with her fist, and foam at the mouth. As her condition deteriorated, her family borrowed money to send her to the hospital, where surgeons removed the rusty 1⅛-in (3-cm) bullet in a four-hour operation. One surgeon said that it was a miracle that she was able to survive for such a long time with a bullet in her head.

### EAR NEST

A pair of spiders made their home in the ear of a nine-year-old boy. When Jesse Courtney of Albany, Oregon, felt a faint popping in his left ear, followed by an ache, doctors flushed out two spiders—one dead, the other alive. Jesse was given the spiders as a souvenir and took them to school to show his friends.

### SWALLOWED HEAD

A man whose head was swallowed by a great white shark managed to break free from the 10-ft (3-m) monster by lunging at its face with a metal chisel. Eric Nerhus, 41, was diving for sea mollusks off the coast of New South Wales, Australia, in January 2007, when the shark grabbed him head-first. It snatched his head, shoulders, and chest into its mouth, but let go after being struck repeatedly with the chisel. Although the surrounding water was red with his blood, Nerhus escaped with a broken nose and deep bite-marks to his chest.

### WEDGED TOOTH

An Australian rugby player carried on playing for more than three months... unaware that he had an opponent's tooth embedded in his forehead. It was only when Ben Czislowski complained of shooting pains that a doctor found the tooth of opposing forward Matt Austin, with whom Czislowski had clashed heads during a match in April 2007.

### QUEASY RIDER

A Japanese motorcyclist carried on riding his bike for more than a mile before realizing that he had lost his leg. The 54-year-old office worker hit a safety barrier but it was only when he stopped a couple of minutes later that he noticed his leg had been severed below the knee.

### PENCIL REMOVAL

A woman in Germany has had part of a pencil removed from her head—after living with it for 55 years. Margaret Wegner was four when she fell over while carrying her pencil. It punctured her cheek and part of it went into her brain, just above her right eye. She has endured nosebleeds and headaches most of her life, but now surgeons in Berlin have managed to remove most of the pencil, although a ½-in (2-mm) section was too deeply embedded for them to get out.

### SPOON SUPPER

A woman accidentally swallowed a spoon 6 in (15 cm) in length while having a laughing fit as she ate a plate of spaghetti in a Sydney, Australia, restaurant in 2007.

### DENTURE DRAMA

A 38-year-old Romanian woman swallowed her lover's false teeth during a passionate kiss. She was rushed to hospital with pains and X rays showed the teeth in her stomach.

## Alien

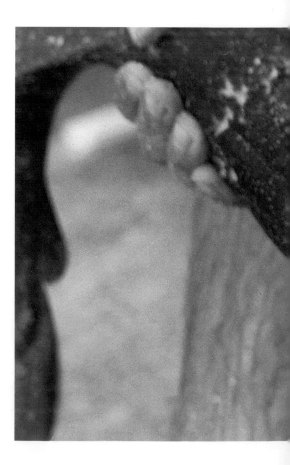

## FACE BUGS

Doctors thought the painful bumps on Aaron Dallas's head might have been gnat bites or shingles... until the bumps started to move. That was when they discovered five botfly larvae living in an ⅛-in-wide (3-mm) pit near the top of his skull. The tiny parasites were probably placed there by a mosquito. "I could feel and hear them," said Dallas of Carbondale, Colorado. "I actually thought I was going crazy."

# Intruders

### Ripley's research...

The botfly is a hairy fly, the larvae of which live as parasites within the bodies of mammals, especially horses. There are about 150 species worldwide, but only one—*Dermatobia hominis*—attacks humans. The female botfly often uses a mosquito to carry her eggs to the host body and when the mosquito bites, the eggs fall off. The heat of the host body induces the larvae to hatch and they then start burrowing into and eating off the flesh for up to eight weeks, before leaving to pupate into an adult fly. They will thrive in any warm part of the body—even in the throat and nose. Since the maggot has strong, hooked spines, it cannot be removed just by squeezing. The best method is either to use a venom extractor syringe or to cover the wound with Vaseline, forcing the maggot up in search of air, and then to pull it out with tweezers.

## SHARK ATTACK

Attacked by a 2-ft (60-cm) shark while he was snorkeling off the coast of New South Wales, Australia, Luke Tresoglavic had to swim 300 yd (275 m) to shore, walk to his car, and drive to a surf club... all with the shark still hanging on to his leg. The Wobbegong shark, which can grow up to 10 ft (3 m) in length, sank its razor-sharp teeth into Tresoglavic's flesh and refused to let go even though lifeguards flushed its gills with fresh water in a bid to loosen its grip. Tresoglavic was treated for puncture wounds to his leg but, sadly, the shark died as a result of the ordeal and was buried in the Tresoglavic family garden.

**MEDICAL MISHAP**

In 2007, a Brazilian woman discovered that the cause of her persistent stomach ache was a 2-in (5-cm) scalpel that had been left in her body when she gave birth by Cesarean section 23 years earlier.

**HIDDEN TOWEL**

When the body of Bonnie Valle from Canton, Ohio, was donated to science after her death in 2002, a green surgical cloth the size of a large hand towel was found behind her left lung. The rolled-up towel had apparently been left there seven years earlier during a surgical procedure on her lungs. Her family said that she had often complained of a funny feeling in her chest.

# A BIG Difference

One of the tallest men in the world at 7 ft 9 in (2.36 m), Bao Xishun shakes hands with fellow Mongolian He Pingping who, at only 2 ft 5 in (73 cm), is less than one-third Bao's height.

Herdsman Bao was of normal size until the age of 16, when he experienced a sudden, unexplained growth spurt, as a result of which he reached his present height just seven years later. In July 2007, after searching the world for a suitable bride, 56-year-old Bao married 5-ft-5-in (1.68-m) Xia Shujuan, a woman from his hometown. She is nearly half his age and more than 2 ft (60 cm) shorter. For the wedding *(see right)*, it took 30 tailors three days to create Bao's outfit.

He Pingping was the size of an adult's palm at birth. Although his two sisters developed normally, he has grown very slowly because of a bone deformity.

*Bao Xishun and Xia Shujuan married in 2007 in traditional Mongolian costume.*

## SHORT & TALL TALES! ▽

| | |
|---|---|
| 1 ft 8 in (51 cm) | Lucia Zarate, Mexico (1864–90). She weighed just 8 oz (227 g) at birth—about the weight of a lemon—and at the age of 12 her waist measured only 14 in (35 cm) in circumference. After finding fame as The Mexican Lilliputian with P.T. Barnum's circus, earning $20 an hour, she died of cold when the train she was on became stuck in a blizzard for a week in the Rocky Mountains. |
| 3 ft 0 in (91 cm) | Michel Petrucciani, France (1962–99). Despite his lack of height, Michel became a brilliant jazz pianist, even though he was so fragile when he was a teenager that he had to be carried to and from the piano. His father made a special extension so that Petrucciani's feet could reach the pedals. |
| 3 ft 4 in (102 cm) | Charles Stratton, Bridgeport, Connecticut, United States (1838–83). Better known as General Tom Thumb, a performer with P.T. Barnum's circus, Stratton married the equally small Lavinia Warren in 1863 and the happy couple stood on top of a grand piano in New York's Metropolitan Hotel to greet 2,000 guests. |
| 8 ft 11 in (2.72 m) | Robert Wadlow, Alton, Illinois, United States (1918–40). Wadlow was 6 ft 2 in (1.88 m) by the age of eight and eventually grew so tall that he had to walk in leg braces. He was buried in a half-ton coffin that had to be carried by 12 pallbearers. |
| 8 ft 9 in (2.67 m) | Eddie Carmel, Bronx, New York City, United States (1936–72). By the time of his death his standing-up height had dropped to 7 ft (2.13 m) owing to the crippling disorder kyphoscoliosis, or curvature of the spine. |
| 8 ft 8 in (2.64 m) | Grady Patterson, DeKalb, Illinois, United States (1943–68). Patterson grew 12 in (30cm) in just one year, aged 13. |

## TALL STORY

At 8 ft 5 in (2.57 m) tall, Leonid Stadnyk, a former veterinarian from the Ukraine, has to sleep on two beds joined together lengthwise. He used to work on a cattle farm but had to quit after suffering frostbite—his feet measure 17 in (43 cm) in length and he could not afford to buy a pair of shoes to fit them. Yet before his growth spurt at age 14, following a brain operation, he was so small that at school he was nicknamed "Titch" (British slang for "a small amount").

### GERMAN GIANT

Known as "Le Géant Constantin," Julius Koch (1872–1902) of Reutlingen, Germany, had hands that measured 15 in (38 cm) long—more than twice the size of an average adult hand. He was believed to be more than 8 ft (2.4 m) tall, but his height had to be estimated because his legs were amputated after developing gangrene.

### UNEQUAL TWINS

Born in Denton, Montana, Donald Koehler (1925–81) experienced an abnormal growth spurt at age ten and stood 8 ft 2 in (2.48 m) tall at his peak. Yet his twin sister was only 5 ft 9 in (1.75 m) tall—a height difference of 29 in (74 cm).

### MIGHTY MING

U.S.-based Chinese basketball player Sun Ming Ming stands 7 ft 9 in (2.36 m) tall and wears size 19 shoes. He did not start playing his sport until he was 15, by which time he was already 6 ft 7 in (2 m) tall.

### TINY TOT

When Edith Barlow of Yorkshire, England, was born in 1925, she weighed just over 1 lb (450 g) and was so tiny that for the first six months of her life she was literally wrapped in cotton wool that had been soaked in olive oil. By the time of her death, at age 25, she had grown to a height of only 1 ft 10 in (55 cm).

### ADMIRAL DOT

Born in San Francisco in 1858, little Leopold Kahn was discovered by showman P.T. Barnum at age four and dubbed "The Eldorado Elf," later renamed as "Admiral Dot." At 16, Kahn was 2 ft 1 in (63 cm) tall, but he eventually reached 4 ft (1.2 m) and became a deputy sheriff and volunteer firefighter in White Plains, New York, making him the smallest man in the United States to hold either post.

### HALF SIZE

When Frenchman Fabien Pretou married Natalie Lucius at Seysinnet-Pariset, France, in 1990, he towered over her in the wedding photos. For he was 6 ft 2 in (1.85 m) tall and she was half his height at 3 ft 1 in (94 cm).

### LONG NOSE

Thomas Wedders, who lived in the U.K. during the 18th century, had a nose that measured 7½ in (19 cm) long. He put his pronounced proboscis to good use by joining a traveling freak show.

# THE HUMAN CANVAS

Chadwick Gray has to remain motionless for up to 15 hours at a time so that artist Laura Spector can paint him. Yet this is no ordinary still life, for the canvas is not a sheet of paper but Chadwick's body.

It is all part of the New York City collaborative team's Museum Anatomy project, which began in 1996 and sees them re-create old paintings onto a human canvas.

Chadwick admits he suffers for his art and enters almost a meditative trance in order to stay completely still for so long. Sometimes his feats of meditative endurance are made publicly. In 2001, for example, Laura painted a 19th-century portrait of a bride onto his body in the front windows of the Henri Bendel department store in New York.

Chadwick and Laura scour the storerooms of museums across the world for likely subjects, frequently looking for paintings that have been stored and hidden away from public view because of their controversial nature. Chadwick says: "We often had to convince conservative curators, and once, in Prague, even a panel of nuns, to allow us to reproduce rare paintings of the female form onto the often naked male body."

Once the body art is completed, Laura photographs Chadwick and the prints are developed to the same size as the original painting. The resulting photographs reveal a new work of art in which the painting acquires curves and sometimes leaves the canvas unrecognizable as Chadwick's human form.

*"Chadwick had to shave his eyebrows for this painting, so the painted lady wouldn't have a mustache. Eyebrows take about three weeks to grow back."*

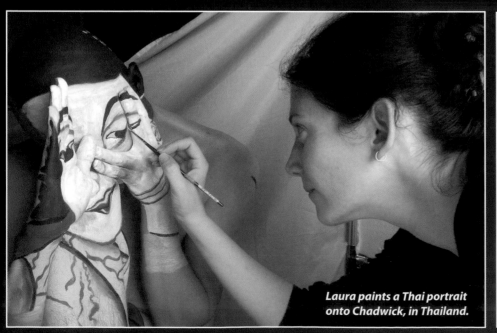

*Laura paints a Thai portrait onto Chadwick, in Thailand.*

*The completed portrait of "Lanna Woman."*

"The original painting from which this was created exists in catacombs underneath a convent in Prague, in the Czech Republic."

"It's rare to find 19th-century portraits in Thailand, so this piece was re-created from the wall of a temple in northern Thailand. The woman represented is the Thai version of Mother Nature—she can water the rice fields with her hair."

"This was our first painting on the body, created in San Francisco, where the painted eye matches up with Chadwick's real eye."

"This painting's original was lost during World War II, so we had to re-create it from a black-and-white photograph."

# Tongue in cheek

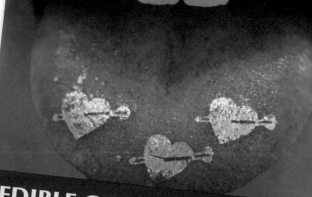

## EDIBLE GOLD

A company in Japan has created edible gold shapes that can float in your coffee or decorate your tongue. As well as offering the height of luxury, the gold is said to help refresh the human body.

**BEE BEARD**

Steve Bryans of Alvinston, Ontario, Canada, had his face crawling with 7,700 bees at an annual bee beard contest at Aylmer, Ontario. The bees, which had been smoked into good behavior, were brushed onto competitors' faces and shaped with feathers into beards. They remained in place because they were attracted by their queens, who were caged and tied around the contestants' necks.

**LONG WASH**

Dae Yu Quin, a 41-year-old woman from Shanghai, China, has hair that is 14 ft 9 in (4.5 m) long. She has not cut it since she was forced to shave her head as a teenager following a scalp disease. It takes her half a day to wash and dry it!

**EYE-POPPING**

Claudio Paulo Pinto of Brazil, can pop his eyeballs out of their sockets a distance of at least 0.3 in (7 mm). He once had a job scaring visitors at a haunted house tourist attraction in Belo Horizonte.

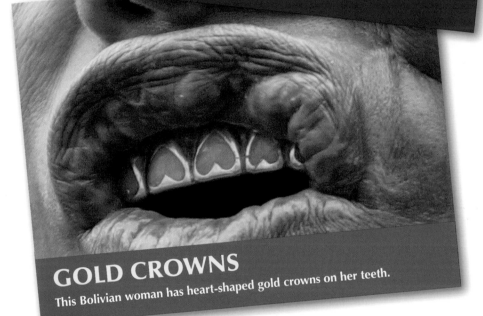

## GOLD CROWNS

This Bolivian woman has heart-shaped gold crowns on her teeth.

# TONGUE TWISTER...

### TOUGH TEETH
Cai Dongsheng of Chongqing City, China, can break nails with his teeth. Protecting his teeth with gauze, he has so far snapped more than 22 lb (10 kg) of nails.

### HICCUP ATTACK
Jennifer Mee of St. Petersburg, Florida, started hiccupping on January 23, 2007, and continued for 38 days straight.

### ALBINO FAMILY
All four children of Canada's Mario and Angie Gaulin were born with albinism, giving them pinkish eyes and white hair.

### TOTAL TATTOO
Lucky Diamond Rich, an Australian performer, has tattoos over every inch of his body—even inside his mouth and ears. Some areas have multiple layers of ink. He has been tattooed by 136 artists in more than 250 studios, in 45 cities and 17 different countries, involving a total tattoo time of 1,150 hours—that's nearly seven weeks.

### LONG NAILS
Li Jianping of Shishi City, China, has let the fingernails on his left hand grow for 15 years—and now they are over 3 ft 3 in (1 m) long. He avoids crowded places and always sleeps with his left wrist under his head to stop that hand from moving.

### MULTIPLE DIGITS
Jeshuah Fuller of New York City was born in August 2007 with six fingers on each hand and six toes on each foot.

### BIG TONGUE
Stephen Taylor of the U.K. has a tongue that is 3.74 in (9.5 cm) long, enabling him to insert it into his nostrils!

### MERMAID EFFECT
A woman from New Zealand with no legs is being fitted with a mermaid's tail so she can pursue her love of swimming. Nadya Vessey had both legs amputated by the age of 16, but has asked the company responsible for the special effects in the Lord of the Rings and King Kong movies to make her a prosthetic tail molded on to a pair of wetsuit shorts.

### FINGER GROWTH
Lee Spievack of Cincinnati, Ohio, lost the tip of a finger in August 2005, but the finger grew back to its original length—and the fingernail on that finger now grows twice as fast as the rest.

### SWOLLEN FINGERS
Liu Hua from Jiangsu Province, China, had fingers that were thicker than his arms. His left thumb, index finger, and middle finger were deformed at birth but grew to an amazing size before surgeons removed 11 lb (5 kg) of bone and tissue in 2007.

### HUMAN BILLBOARD
Edson Alves from Tanabi, Brazil, makes a living by having advertisements tattooed on his body. He walks around with his shirt off, displaying more than 20 tattoos promoting local shops, restaurants, and businesses.

## TONGUE SPLITTING

James Keen from Scottsville, Kentucky, shows off his split tongue. He had it split by a piercer using a scalpel heated by a blowtorch and no anesthetic. Although it is said to enhance the pleasure of kissing, the practice is now illegal in some U.S. states, where it is considered tantamount to mutilation.

Mohammed Rafi of Kerala, India, can twist his tongue at a 180-degree angle and roll it inside out by flipping his entire tongue backward. He can touch the tip of his nose with his tongue and can also roll it into all sorts of shapes—a flower, a shell, and even a boat.

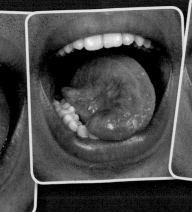
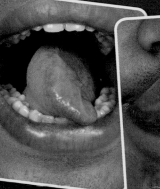
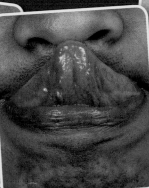
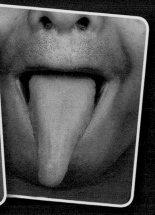

## BRIEF AWAKENING

A woman awoke from a six-year coma—but only for three days. Christa Lilly had been in a coma in Colorado Springs, Colorado, since suffering a heart attack and stroke in late 2000. Then, in 2007, she suddenly woke up and started talking to doctors and family, although she believed it was 1986. However, three days later she mysteriously lapsed back into a vegetative state.

## SWEET TASTE

Humans with a particularly acute sense of taste are able to detect sweetness in a solution that is one part sugar to 200 parts water. In comparison, certain moths and butterflies can detect sweetness when the ratio is one part sugar to 300,000 parts water.

## LANGUAGE CONFUSION

After being knocked unconscious in a speedway race in Glasgow, Scotland, Czech driver Matej Kus came round and started talking perfect English—even though he could barely speak the language before he had the accident! His newfound language skills did not last, however, and when he had recovered he could once again speak only broken English.

## NO PULSE

Gerard Langevin of Quebec, Canada, was fitted with a new heart but now he has no pulse!

## SECOND LIVER

Jenna Hopkins of Crab Orchard, Kentucky, was born with a second liver growing in her right lung.

## PHONE LIGHT

As a result of a power failure, surgeons at a hospital in Villa Mercedes, Argentina, had to finish an operation using the light emitted by cell phones.

## CELL NUMBERS

Our galaxy has more than 100 billion stars, but a human body has about 100 trillion cells.

## POWERFUL PUMP

The human heart creates enough pressure when it pumps blood out into the body to squirt blood a distance of 30 ft (9 m).

## MOSQUITO SWARM

It would take approximately 1.2 million mosquitoes to drain an average human being of all of their blood.

## RARE BLOOD

The rarest blood group in the world is a type of Bombay blood known as H-H. It was first discovered in Bombay in 1950, and it is thought that only 57 people in the whole of India have it.

## BRICK BITE

The muscles on the sides of a human mouth allow you to bite into things with a force of 160 lb (72.5 kg)—equivalent to the weight of 35 house bricks.

## HUGE HAIRBALL

An 18-year-old from Chicago, Illinois, had a huge hairball weighing 10 lb (4.5 kg) and measuring 15 in (38 cm) long removed from her stomach in 2007. The teenager, who had a habit of eating her hair, complained to doctors of pains in her stomach—where they later found a mass of black, curly hair.

## BACTERIA MASS

There are 516,000 bacteria per square inch in a human armpit.

# THE BLUE MAN

A man from California has skin that is permanently blue. Paul Karason of Madera developed the condition 15 years ago after using a homemade silver remedy to treat dermatitis on his face. Despite the unfortunate side effect, he swears by its powers and has even got used to his nickname of Papa Smurf.

## Ripley's research

Suffering from stress-related dermatitis after his father's death, Paul Karason decided to treat it with his own mixture of colloidal silver, a medicine widely used before the discovery of penicillin. However, silver has been banned in U.S. medicines since 1999 because it causes argyria, a condition that turns the skin blue. He probably exacerbated the problem by rubbing the silver into the peeling skin on his face as well as taking it orally.

# MIRACLE WALKER

Born with spina bifida, by the age of 34 Mark Chenoweth was resigned to spending the rest of his life in a wheelchair. Doctors told him he would never walk again.

Then, on holiday in Menorca in 1998, against the advice of his doctor, he persuaded a dive center to let him go scuba diving for the first time. He plunged to a depth of 55 ft (17 m)—and when he emerged from the water he found that he could walk again.

"It was just unbelievable," says Mark. "I came out and I could feel my legs like I had never felt them before. They were actually working. The instructor couldn't believe it. He'd seen me arrive in my wheelchair, and now I didn't need it."

Three days later his legs became lifeless again, but back home in Staffordshire, England, he quickly booked his next diving holiday. Since then he has found that the deeper he dives, the longer he can walk for afterward. As a result he now needs his wheelchair only twice a year.

| DEPTH DIVED | WALKING PERIOD AFTERWARD |
|---|---|
| 55 ft (17 m) | 3–4 days |
| 100 ft (30 m) | 2–3 months |
| 130 ft (40 m) | 4 months |
| 165 ft (50 m) | 8 months |

## Ripley's research

The deeper divers go, the richer the mix of oxygen that they take in from their aqualungs, and one theory is that this extra oxygen is affecting the nerve cells damaged by Mark's spina bifida and is making them temporarily work.

## SPOON SURGERY

In 1942, Wheeler Lipes, a 23-year-old crewman in the U.S. Navy, performed an emergency appendectomy on another crew member using only spoons as retractors and a scalpel blade with no handle. Lipes was not even a doctor—he was a pharmacist's mate—and he carried out the successful operation on a submarine that was cruising 120 ft (36 m) under the South China Sea!

## IRON RESOURCE

If all the iron in the human body were gathered together, there would be enough to make a medium-sized nail.

# PREMATURE BABY

Born at Miami, Florida, in October 2006, little Amillia Sonja Taylor survived despite a gestation period of fewer than 22 weeks. She spent 21 weeks 6 days in the womb (full-term births are between 37 and 40 weeks) and at birth weighed less than 10 oz (284 g) and measured just 9½ in (24 cm) long—that's only slightly longer than a ballpoint pen.

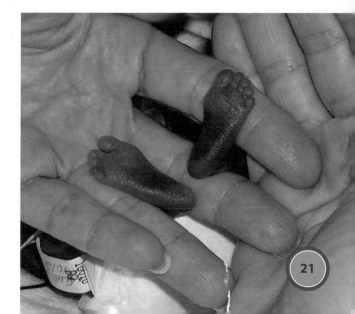

## PIERCING RECORD

Brent Moffatt from Winnipeg, Canada, pierced himself with 900 surgical needles in 2003 in an effort to break his previous body-piercing record of 702.

### CURVED HORN

A Chinese grandmother has a 5-in (13-cm) horn growing out of her forehead. Ninety-five-year-old Granny Zhao of Zhanjiang City, says the horn, which curves downward and looks like the stalk of a pumpkin, grew from a mole three years ago. It causes her no pain but interferes slightly with her vision.

### GREEN BLOOD

Surgeons operating on a 42-year-old man in Vancouver, British Columbia, Canada, were alarmed to discover that he had green blood! Tests revealed that he had taken too many doses of a headache pill, which had caused his blood to change color.

### LOUD SNAP

Robert Hatch of Pasadena, California, snaps his fingers at a sound level of 108 decibels—almost as loud as a rock concert.

### NECK TUMOR

Seventeen years after first discovering a strange growth on the back of his neck, 58-year-old Huang Liqian of Chongqing, China, finally had it removed in 2007. In that time it had grown into a huge neck tumor weighing an incredible 33 lb (15 kg).

**Egg on Face!**

A British man has a tattoo of a full English breakfast on the top of his head. Dayne Gilbey from Coventry sports a tattoo of bacon, sausages, eggs, beans, and even cutlery. Tattooist Blane Dickinson, who carried out the six-hour artwork, said he now wants to find someone willing to have their face tattooed on the back of their head.

### MAGIC TRICK
Actor Daniel Radcliffe, best known for his role as Harry Potter in the movies of the same name, can hold his hand on a flat surface and rotate it 360 degrees.

### ABDOMINAL GROWTH
Chen Huanxiang of Wuhan, China, was admitted to a hospital in April 2007 for the removal of a whopping 110-lb (50-kg) abdominal tumor.

### PIZZA HEAD
To mark the opening of his takeout pizza shop, Colin Helsby of Penmaenmawr, Wales, had a slice of ham-and-pineapple pizza tattooed on the back of his head. The tattooist took three hours to complete the artwork, which features three types of ham, chunks of pineapple, and strands of cheese dripping down Helsby's neck.

### RARE CASE
Lydia Fairchild of Washington State, is one of only 50 people in the world known to be born with two different sets of DNA, a condition known as "chimerism." Doctors made the discovery in 2002 when she had to prove that she was her chidren's mother.

### SHOCK DISCOVERY
Chinese surgeons operating on a 10-month-old baby girl from Zhoukou found grass growing on her right lung. The 1³/₁₆-in (3-cm) piece of grass was the same type as in the yard at home where she often plays. Doctors say it is possible that grass seed was blown into the baby's nose and through her respiratory system to the lung, where it found suitable growing conditions.

### REPLACEMENT HORN
A man in the Yemen has grown two horns. Saleh, aged 102, had often dreamed he was growing a horn on his head and one finally sprouted on the left side 25 years ago. It grew to 1 ft 8 in (50 cm) before falling off but a second one has now grown in its place.

### PARASITIC DRESS
Born in Albany, Georgia, in 1932, performer Betty Lou Williams had a parasitic twin protruding from the front of her torso. The twin consisted of two legs, one arm with three fingers, and a second arm that was little more than a single finger. Sometimes she dressed the twin in tiny clothes and off-stage she kept it hidden under a maternity dress.

### LONG FINGER
Before surgery, Liu Hua of Jiangsu, China, had an index finger on his left hand that was 12 in (30 cm) long.

### LEG BATTLE
Two men were feuding in 2007 over who had the rightful ownership of a severed leg. John Wood of Greenville, South Carolina, had the leg amputated after a plane crash, but kept it in a barbecue smoker so that he could be buried "whole" when he died. However, the smoker containing the leg was among items that Shannon Whisnant of Maiden, North Carolina, bought at an auction—and he wanted to keep it.

### SUPERSIZE CYST
When Taquela Hilton of Kellyville, Oklahoma, ballooned to more than 560 lb (254 kg) with a 71-in (180-cm) waist, doctors thought that she was eating too much. Instead, the cause of her weight-gain was a 93-lb (42-kg) ovarian cyst, containing 12 gal (45 l) of fluid. After removing the cyst, one surgeon said: "This was like having a C-section to deliver a 12-year-old. It was a small adult that she was carrying around in her."

# EIGHT-LIMBED GIRL

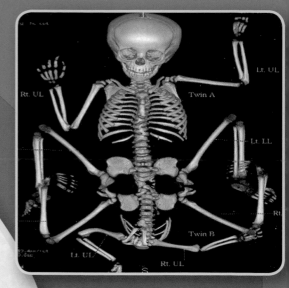

A girl born in India with four arms and four legs had the extra limbs removed in a groundbreaking 27-hour operation. Shortly afterward, she was able to stand up and walk for the first time in her life.

Lakshmi Tatma was born a conjoined twin in the impoverished northern state of Bihar. In a rare condition called isciopagus, her twin had stopped developing in the mother's womb and the surviving fetus had absorbed the parasitic twin's limbs, kidneys, and other body parts. Although the twin had a torso and limbs, it had no head and its body was joined to Lakshmi's at the pelvis.

So Lakshmi, who was named after the four-armed Hindu goddess of wealth, was born with two spines, four kidneys, entangled nerves, two stomach cavities, two chest cavities, four arms, and four legs. Many local people revered her as a goddess and lined up for a blessing from the child, but her father, Shambhu, was forced to keep her in hiding after a circus tried to buy her.

In November 2007, the two-year-old underwent an operation at a hospital in Bangalore. As well as removing the surplus limbs, surgeons transplanted a kidney from Lakshmi's twin into her own body, moved her bowels and intestines into a more central position, and amputated the headless twin altogether.

Afterward, when Lakshmi was able to stand up to reach her favorite toy, her mother, Poonam, said: "I had tears in my eyes, it was a dream I thought would never happen."

### CHAIR ATTACK

An X ray shows a metal chair leg lodged in Shafique el-Fahkri's left eye socket following a fight outside a nightclub in Melbourne, Australia. When the chair was thrown at el-Fahkri, the leg penetrated his eye socket, moving his eyeball to the side, and speared down into his neck. Incredibly, he has recovered 95 percent of his vision, although the incident has left him with a raspy voice.

### ROBOTIC LEGS

Peng Shulin of China lost his lower body in a 1995 truck accident, but 12 years later doctors in Beijing gave him robotic legs.

### REATTACHED LIMB

Israel Sarrio of Valencia, Spain, had his arm severed during an accident in January 2004 and doctors sewed it to his leg to keep it alive until they could reattach it properly.

### TIMELY RECOVERY

Carlos Camejo of Venezuela was declared dead following a car accident in September 2007, but awoke during his autopsy as the coroner began to cut him!

### INTERNAL DECAPITATION

Shannon Malloy survived a car crash in which her skull was separated from her spine—a condition called internal decapitation. At a special surgical unit in Denver, Colorado, doctors drilled five screws into her neck and four into her head to reattach it. Then she was fitted with a metal halo—which consists of rods and a circular bar—to keep her head stabilized, but even during the fitting of the halo her unattached head kept slipping off her neck.

### SCISSORS FOUND

In November 2006, doctors found surgical scissors in the abdomen of a woman from Thenpattinam, India. The scissors had been there for 12 years—ever since a previous operation on the woman in 1994.

### BROKEN NECK

Fourteen-year-old sports fanatic Alfie Tyson-Brown of Dorset, England, led an active life for 10 years—unaware that he had a broken neck that could have killed him at any time. He played rugby, surfed, went mountain biking, and rode roller coasters before doctors finally discovered his life-threatening injury.

### IMPALEMENT HORROR

Ezra Bias of Spokane, Washington, miraculously survived after being impaled through the head by a 2-ft-long (60-cm) piece of steel bar. He was delivering pizza when a car drove over the bar as it lay in the road, flipping it up into the air, from where if flew through Bias' windshield and into his head.

### PROSTHETIC ARMS

Jesse Sullivan of Dayton, Tennessee, has a pair of amazing prosthetic arms that he is able to move merely by thinking about their movement!

### HIDDEN GLASS

Xiao Zhu of China wondered why he always kept crying from one eye—until doctors found that he had had a 1⅓-in-long (3.5-cm) piece of glass buried under his right eye for the past six years. The eye had been injured in a fight, but the operation to repair the injury had missed the shard of glass.

### MIRACLE CURE

Frazer Simpson of Northumberland, England, was accidentally splashed in the face with a corrosive chemical and, rather than hurting his eyes, it miraculously improved his eyesight to the point where he no longer needed glasses to drive.

## MASSIVE TUMOR

A medical technician at a hospital in Belgrade, Serbia, holds a huge tumor removed from the abdomen of a 54-year-old woman. The benign tumor weighed 86 lb (39 kg)—that's the weight of an average 11-year-old! Amazingly, the woman survived.

# Enter the Vault

## LITTLE AND LARGE
Extremes of tall and short people from West (left) and East (right) seen in the 1930s and 1880s respectively.

## BITE ME!
This oyster shell grew up around an old set of missing false teeth!

## CRANIAL HOPPER
In 1931, Alexandre Patty's party trick was to ascend staircases "walking" on his head! He called the technique "cranial hopping."

## SAY WHAT?
Max Calvin, from Brooklyn, New York, never needed to fish for change. He could hold an astonishing 25 quarters in his ear!

## CONJOINED TWINS
This photograph of conjoined twins, Mary and Arrita, was taken in 1924. The girls, from Mexico City, Mexico, were joined at the ribcage.

## ON THE CHIN

Robert Dotzauer of Davenport, Iowa, was able to balance two heavy iron lawn mowers on his chin.

## SUPERSIZE ME!

At one point, both Sam Harris of Farmersville, Texas, and Alice Dunbar of Dallas, Texas, were the heaviest man and woman alive, weighing 691 lb (313 kg) and 685 lb (311 kg) respectively.

**SAM HARRIS**
TEX-KID
FARMERSVILLE, TEXAS
HEAVIEST MAN LIVING. WEIGHT 691 LBS.

Weight 685#

## HORIZONTAL STRENGTH ▼

Laurence J. Frankel was able to hold himself horizontally on stall bars with a 110-lb (50-kg) weight attached to his back.

## ◄ A REAL MOUTHFUL

Despite standing a mere 5 ft (1.52 m) in height, Jackie del Rio of Chicago, Illinois, managed to lift two tables and six chairs—with his teeth!

## HUMAN FLAG ▲

Perry L. Biddle of DeFuniack Springs, Florida, is seen here performing his human flag impersonation on his 90th birthday in 1936.

## SAND REMEDY

*Patients in Thailand travel from far and wide to be buried up to their necks in hot sand and then stood on by a doctor. They flock to the northeastern province of Buriram to be treated by witch doctor Pan Rerngprasarn, who believes ancient Cambodian healing can cure anything from cancer to mental illness.*

### HALF BRAIN

A 39-year-old woman from Wuhan, China, has lived a normal life despite having only half a brain. Although scans showed no gray matter on the left side—the part of the brain that controls language—she has no problem communicating with people.

### STRETCHED EARS

The witch doctor of the Kuria tribe in Tanzania, Africa, used to stretch his ear lobes until they were so large that a child could be passed through them—an act believed to cure the children of their ailments.

### HEART STOPPING

Three-time New York City Marathon champion Alberto Salazar survived a heart attack at Beaverton, Oregon, in 2007—even though his heart stopped beating for a whopping 16 minutes.

### BEAR NECESSITY

In 16th-century Europe, a cure for fainting was to take fur from the belly of a live bear, boil it in alcohol, and place it on the soles of the ailing person's feet.

### HEALING GRAVE

Locals say that graves in a churchyard at Launceston, England, can cure a stiff neck if, on May 1, 2, or 3, the ailing person applies dew from a newly dug grave to their neck.

### CANCER CURE

In 1588, Jean Nicot, France's ambassador to Portugal, sent tobacco plants to his homeland in the belief that tobacco was a cure for cancer.

### WRONG LEG

Surgeons in China trying to correct the limp of a five-year-old boy accidentally lengthened the wrong leg. They said the mistake was due to the boy being anesthetized on his back but then operated on while lying on his stomach. As a result, he had to undergo two more operations—one to extend his right leg, the other to shorten his wrongly extended left leg.

### TWO WOMBS

At a hospital in Bristol, England, in December 2006, Hannah Kersey gave birth to three children from two different wombs. Identical twins Ruby and Tilly were delivered from one womb and a single baby, Grace, was delivered from the other. Kersey was born with an unusual condition called uterus didelphus, which leads to the abnormal development of the reproductive organs.

### MISTAKEN IDENTITY

In October 2007, after overseeing the cremation of a man she thought was her son, a woman was shocked when he turned up alive the next day. Gina Partington had identified a body found in Manchester, England, as her 39-year-old son Thomas Dennison, but 24 hours later he was found alive and well 85 mi (137 km) away in Nottingham.

### SNAKE BITE

Matt Wilkinson of Portland, Oregon, spent three days in a coma in 2007 after putting his 20-in (51-cm) pet diamondback rattlesnake into his mouth. He made it to the hospital just in time, as his airway had nearly swollen shut from the venomous bites.

## FIERY TREATMENT

Walnuts and ignited dry moxa leaves are placed on a patient's eyes in Jinan, China, as treatment for eye disease. Taken from the plant *Artemisia chinensis*, burned moxa leaves are a staple ingredient of Traditional Chinese Medicine.

### IMPALED ON SPIKE

A five-year-old boy from Sydney, Australia, survived after being speared through the throat by an iron-fence spike in July 2007. The spike plunged 2 in (5 cm) into the throat of Hugo Borbilas, narrowly missing his carotid artery, esophagus, windpipe, all the major nerves in his neck and throat, and stopping just short of his brain. The injury could have killed Hugo instantly, but he managed to pull himself off the spike and yell for help.

### VODKA DRIP

Doctors in the city of Brisbane in Queensland, Australia, attached a poisoned Italian tourist to a vodka drip in 2007 after running out of supplies of the medicinal alcohol they normally use.

### RABID RECOVERY

Teenager Jeanna Giese of Fond Du Lac, Wisconsin, had to relearn how to walk, talk, and function after catching rabies from a bat bite in September 2004. It took more than a year for her to be able to walk unaided, but she still graduated highschool with honors in 2007. Jeanna is thought to be the only person ever to have survived the deadly disease, which attacks the nervous system, without having had a vaccination.

### HOLY SNAIL

The Church of St. Leonard in the medieval town of Guingamp, France, was visited for centuries by people from Brittany in the belief they could cure a fever by finding a snail in a cavity in the church walls and carrying it in a pouch.

### DINOSAUR MEDICINE

Villagers in China have spent decades digging up dinosaur bones for use in medicine. The calcium-rich bones are boiled with other ingredients and fed to children to treat dizziness and leg cramps. They are also ground into a paste and then applied directly to wounds to help heal bone fractures.

### FROG IN THE THROAT

Ancient Romans would cure toothaches by holding a frog boiled in water and vinegar inside the mouth of the patient.

### NEW GRADUATE

Maurice Yankow of Valhalla, New York, enrolled in medical school at age 63—and became a practising licensed physician at 70 years of age.

# MUDDY BEAUTY

Visitors to a resort in China's Sichuan Province cover themselves from head to toe in black mud. The mineral-rich mud is said to be beneficial to the skin.

# TILL DEATH DO US PART

## WELL-TRAVELED BRAIN

When Princeton pathologist Dr. Thomas Harvey performed the autopsy on Albert Einstein in 1955, he chose to remove the physicist's brain. He later had it cut into 240 pieces, which he kept in two jars stored inside a cider box at his various homes across America. From time to time he sent pieces to researchers.

In 1997, Harvey traveled to meet Einstein's granddaughter in California and took the brain with him in the trunk of his car. He accidentally left the brain at her house but she did not want it, so the following year she sent it back to Princeton.

## WHERE THE HEART IS

Famous English poet and novelist Thomas Hardy (1840–1928) wanted to be buried in the village of Stinsford—his birthplace—in the picturesque English county of Dorset. When he died, however, his wife was offered the great honor of him being buried in "Poet's Corner" in London's great Westminster Abbey. To resolve the dilemma, his wife decided that his heart would be buried at Stinsford and his ashes interred in the Abbey.

## HARMONIOUS HAIR

When Ludwig van Beethoven died in 1827, this lock of his hair was taken from his head as a keepsake of the great German composer. It became the property of the Royal Philharmonic Society in London, England, almost a hundred years later, and now belongs to the British Library.

## HITLER'S HEAD
What are believed to be Adolf Hitler's skull and jaw are stored at the Federal Archives Service in Moscow, Russia. The skull piece is stored on two sheets of tissue in a floppy disk container. Ironically, Hitler had ordered a German officer to burn his remains because he didn't want to end up on display in the Soviet Union.

## ARTIFICIAL LEGS
The artificial legs of British World War II fighter pilot Douglas Bader are on display at the R.A.F. Museum in Stafford, England. Bader heroically flew in the Battle of Britain despite losing both of his legs in a plane crash 11 years earlier.

## HANDS APART
Body parts from 16th-century Spanish missionary St. Francis Xavier were in such demand as relics that they are now scattered all over the globe. His left hand is in Cochin, India, while his right is in Malacca, Malaysia.

## MISSING ARM
British Admiral Horatio Nelson's right arm is said to be kept in the cathedral in Las Palmas, Gran Canaria. It was amputated after being shattered by grapeshot during an assault on Tenerife in 1797.

## AMPUTATED LEG
Even though his right leg was nearly blown off by a cannonball during the Battle of Gettysburg, Dan Sickles calmly smoked a cigar on his way to the medical tent. After the leg was amputated, Sickles donated it to the Army Medical Museum, where he would later take friends to impress them with his bravery.

## MACABRE WARNING
Oliver Cromwell died in 1658, but three years later the reinstated English monarchy under King Charles II exhumed his body and had him posthumously executed. His head was then impaled on a pike in Westminster Hall, where it remained for 20 years as a warning to others. The head now rests in a chapel in Cambridge, England.

## SPINAL COLUMN
Twelve days after murdering President Abraham Lincoln, John Wilkes Booth was fatally shot in the neck. His body was later buried in an unmarked grave in Baltimore but his third, fourth, and fifth vertebrae had already been removed during the autopsy to gain access to the bullet. These parts of his spinal column are on display at the National Museum of Health and Medicine in Washington, D.C.

## ELVIS'S WART
Joni Mabe, "the Elvis Babe," of Cornelia, Georgia, keeps Elvis Presley's wart in a tube of formaldehyde. She bought the wart—part of her collection of Elvis memorabilia—in 1990 from a Memphis doctor who had removed it from Elvis's right wrist when Presley joined the army in 1958.

## LINCOLN RELICS
Part of President Abraham Lincoln's skull is housed at the National Museum of Health and Medicine in Washington, D.C. Also displayed are bits of his hair and the bullet that killed him.

## BODY SNATCHERS
After Catherine of Siena died in 1380, pilgrims came to visit her body from all over Europe in the belief that touching it would cure their illnesses. One over-zealous worshiper removed one of Catherine's fingers and Pope Urban VI took her head.

## PRESIDENTIAL TUMOR
President Grover Cleveland's tumor is kept in a jar at the Mütter Museum, Philadelphia, Pennsylvania. It was removed from the roof of his mouth in a secret operation.

# FINGER OF DISCOVERY
Italian physicist Galileo (1564–1642) is credited with being the founding father of modern science. In 1737, the middle finger on his right hand was removed when his body was moved from its original grave to a mausoleum in the Santa Croce church in Florence, Italy. It eventually became the property of Florence's Institute and Museum of the History of Science in 1927, where it is now on display. The finger symbolizes how Galileo's work pointed the way toward modern science.

# TOOTH TRUTH

Laser scans performed on George Washington's teeth at the National Museum of Dentistry in Baltimore in 2005 showed that they were not made of wood as was commonly believed. Instead, his dentures turned out to be made from gold, ivory, lead, and human and animal teeth (probably horse and donkey). The dentures had springs to help them open and were held together by bolts.

## COCKROACH TEA

In Louisiana in the 1800s, a tea made using cockroaches was a remedy for tetanus, while cockroaches fried in oil with garlic were used as a cure for indigestion.

## STONE DOCTOR

A statue that was covered with magical inscriptions was used for centuries by the ancient Egyptians as a cure for snakebite and scorpion stings. The patient would pour water over the statue and then drink it.

## HAIR SANDWICH

To cure a cough in medieval England, a hair from the cougher's head was placed in a bread-and-butter sandwich and fed to a dog.

## PROLONGED PREGNANCY

An X ray on a 90-year-old woman in Sichuan, China, revealed that she had been pregnant for 58 years. When doctors examined the old lady, they found a dead, distorted fetus in her uterus, dating back to 1949 when she had a still birth.

## LUCKY LOOK

Women in China undergo cosmetic surgery to look lucky. They ask for less prominent cheekbones, which are said to bring bad luck to their husbands, or to have small blemishes removed from around the eyes or mouth because they, too, are considered unlucky.

## WORM TEA

Chong Cha, a Chinese black tea made from the droppings of certain caterpillars, is drunk to prevent heatstroke. Popularly known as worm tea, it is also claimed to help with diarrhea, nosebleeds, and hemorrhoids.

## BEAUTY TREATMENT

Drinking the saliva of small birds called swiftlets is said to promote beautiful skin for women in China. The saliva is collected from the binding material of the birds' nests, which are then cleaned and cooked in water.

## WIZARD LIZARD

The spiny-tailed iguana is eaten in the Sierra Madre Mountains of Mexico as a cure for depression.

## EGG REMEDY

An American cure for lowering fever is to soak two cloths in egg whites and put them on the soles of the feet. The egg whites immediately start to draw the temperature down from the brain to the feet.

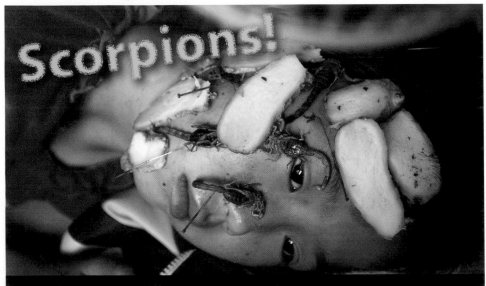

*Dead scorpions and slices of ginger are laid on a patient's face in China in an attempt to cure facial paralysis.*

## SOME AGE-OLD CURES

🐛 Passing a child three times under the belly of a donkey cures whooping cough.

🐛 Extracting the tooth of a live mole and wearing it cures toothaches.

🐛 Binding the temples with a rope with which a man has been hanged relieves a headache.

🐛 Urinating in an open grave is a remedy for incontinence.

🐛 Carrying a dead shrew in your pocket wards off rheumatism.

🐛 To cure tuberculosis, put your head into the carcass of a freshly slaughtered cow while the body is still steaming, draw the folds of flesh around your neck, and inhale.

## TOOTHBRUSH TREE

Instead of brushing their teeth, some African tribes in Chad and the Sudan chew on sticks carved from the wood of the *Salvadora persica*, or "toothbrush tree." The wood releases a bacteria-fighting liquid that helps prevent infection and tooth decay.

## SWALLOW PLEASE!

A cure for dizziness in 16th-century England was to take a young swallow from its nest during a crescent moon, cut off the bird's head, allowing the blood to run into a vessel containing frankincense, and give the potion to the patient when the moon was waning.

## WART REMEDY

A popular cure for warts was once to put a piece of silver and some rocks in a small sack by the side of the road, in the belief that whoever took the sack would also take the warts. Another wart remedy was to steal a steak and bury it where three roads crossed.

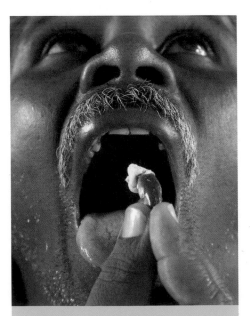

# OPEN WIDE!

**Live fish dipped in medicinal paste are claimed to be a cure for asthma in parts of India.**

### PEE POWER
In many parts of Asia, people believe that drinking your own urine cures a variety of ailments—including snakebites, heart disease, chicken pox, infertility, and baldness. Some Japanese women even bathe in their own urine as part of their beauty regime—to improve their skin.

### SHEEP'S EYE
In Outer Mongolia, a cure for a hangover consists of eating a pickled sheep's eye in a glass of tomato juice.

### ASTHMA CURE
The Chinese believe that eating dried seahorses will cure impotence and asthma. Two tons of seahorses are used each year in the Chinese medicine trade.

### BUFFALO DRIVE
The cure for any plague that besets the Bhar tribesmen of India is to drive a black water buffalo out of their village—in the belief that it will carry away the disease.

### DANCE ROUTINE
The cure for any illness among the Betsileo tribesmen of Madagascar is to put the patient into a trance and then order him to rise from his bed and dance. After a week of this treatment the patient is usually cured—or dead!

### MIXED SOUP
A soup made from herbs and Taiwanese tree lizards is believed to be good for asthma and colds. The cure is apparently most effective when one male and one female lizard are used in the soup.

### COW TEA
An unusual cold remedy in the southern states of the United States is to drink tea made from dried cow manure.

### SWEEPING DIAGNOSIS
Nigerians believe that a man hit with a broom will become impotent unless he retaliates by hitting the hitter seven times with the same broom.

### ORANGE CURE
Sara Jane Trout of Aspinwall, Pennsylvania, ate 3,248 oranges in 1938 as a cure for diabetes.

### BITTER LESSON
Some people insist that putting earwax in your mouth can help to ease toothache—apparently it numbs the area that is hurting.

## FROGS ALIVE!
Jiang Musheng from China has been eating live frogs to cure his coughs for 40 years.

## ACKNOWLEDGMENTS

COVER (t/r) Chadwick and Spector www.chadwickandspector.com, (b/r) Manichi Rafi; 4 Chadwick and Spector www.chadwickandspector.com;
6 (bgd) Alex Pang, (b) CNImaging/Photoshot; 6-7 (sp, c) Zhang Xiuke/ChinaPhotoPress/Photocome/PA Photos; 8 (t) Amia Fore, (b) AFP/
Getty Images; 9 ChinaFotoPress/Wang Zi/Photocome/PA Photos; 10–11 www.anilgupta.com; 12 (t/l, t/c) Newscom/Wenn; 13 (t/r) Kelley
Cox/AP/PA Photos, (t/l) Stephen Krasemann/NHPA/Photoshot; 12–13 (c) Reuters/Stringer Australia; 14 (t) Reuters/Jason Lee, (b) AP/PA
Photos; 15 Wojtek Laski/Rex Features; 16 (t, b/l, b/r) Chadwick and Spector www.chadwickandspector.com, (t) Studio-54/Fotolia.com;
17 (t/l, t/r, b/l, b/r) Chadwick and Spector www.chadwickandspector.com, (t/l) Philip Hunton/Fotolia.com, (t/r) Aleksander Yurovskikh/
Fotolia.com, (b/l) catnap/Fotolia.com, (b/r) Kirill Zdorov/Fotolia.com; 18 (t) Reuters/Kim Kyung Hoon, (c) Reuters/Marcos Brindicci, (b)
Manichi Rafi; 19 (t) Joe Imel/AP/PA Photos, (b) Manichi Rafi; 20 NBCUPhotobank/Rex Features; 21 (t) Gary Roberts/Rex Features, (b)
Reuters/Ho New; 22 (t) Reuters/Shaun Best, (b/l, b/r) Peter Byrne/PA Archive/PA Photos; 23 Peter Byrne/PA Archive/PA Photos;
24 (t/l, t/r) AP/PA Photos, (b) Aijaz Rahi/AP/PA Photos; 25 Reuters/STR New; 28 (t) Reuters/Apichart Weerawong, (b) Reuters/Stringer
Shanghai; 29 Reuters/China Daily China Daily Information Corp – CDIC; 30 (b/l) Peter Macdiarmid/Rex Features, (b) Steve Pyke/Getty
Images; 31 (l) Keith Srakocic/AP/PA Photos, (r) Institute and Museum of the History of Science, Italy; 32 (t) Reuters/Stringer Shanghai,
(b) Reuters/Stringer India; 33 Reuters/China Daily China Daily Information Corp - CDIC

Key: t = top, b = bottom, c = center, l = left, r = right, sp = single page, dp = double page

All other photos are from Ripley Entertainment Inc.
Every attempt has been made to acknowledge correctly and contact copyright holders and we apologize in advance for any unintentional errors
or omissions, which will be corrected in future editions.